S

AVED

INGLE &

OLIDIFIED
In Christ

Lorraine Hopkins

Saved, Single, & Solidified in Christ

Cover Designed and Illustrations by Lorraine Hopkins
SAVED, SINGLE, & SOLIDIFIED IN CHRIST

Copyright © 2015 by Lorraine Hopkins
Library of Congress Control Number: TX0008113531

Published By: Keeping Our Lights Lit Ministries
Printed in USA by 48HrBooks (www.48HrBooks.com)
ISBN: 978-1-943396-00-9

Author: Lorraine Hopkins
Editor: Cornette Barfield

All Biblical Scriptures came from the New King James Version of the Holy Bible, unless otherwise noted.
All definitions came from Merriam-Webster Dictionary Online.

Dedication

"I dedicate this book to every single person, who has made a decision to live a holy and righteous life in Christ Jesus! Do not get weary in well doing because you shall reap if you faint not. Always remember, God will not tempt you beyond what you can bear, and He always provides a way of escape. God bless you. I love you but remember there is no greater love than that of our Father! "

— Lorraine Hopkins

Table of Contents

Foreword

When Lorraine asked me to write the foreword for her latest work; I was surely honored, because I have never been asked to complete such a task. Eventually, anxiety set in. Why me? I am not an author of any kind, I thought. How do I write this? What am I supposed to say? Even if I do a good job, will anyone read it? I have seen forewords in books, and I have to admit that the most love I will show it is to skim through it. Then I thought about it even deeper, as I always do. I said, well maybe she asked me because she knows I could give the best depiction of her story and the work it took to complete it.

I have seen Lorraine write books time and time again; wondering how someone always comes up with so much fresh material. She is writing books and completing her master's degree at the same time. I started thinking, how often are you getting writer's block woman! There were so many long nights of her running ideas past me, to see if things make sense in the context, she had them in. It was usually right, but I guess when you look at things in the early morning hours while you are tired, it might make you a little delirious.

How about popping up in the middle of the night because you're dreaming of the words to be written and jotting down thoughts and ideas at times she should be sleeping. If only I had a quarter for every time she asked, "What you think about this?" (Laughing to myself) There are times we would be in the middle of a conversation and suddenly the topic ends because thoughts and ideas have surfaced to the forefront of her mind. Then she says, "wait a minute, I better jot this down before I lose it." Leaving me looking at the phone like, where are these random ideas coming from? Yet, anyone that knows Lorraine, understands this is how she operates. She will never let an idea go wasted because her brain is constantly in motion.

In Saved, Single, and Solidified in Christ; Lorraine is giving you all of her. She shares some of her struggle in walking the path of righteousness and trying to live in a Christ like manner, while still battling internal forces and people, trying to persuade her to do otherwise. She lets you in, showing herself in a light that makes her transparent to the reader and allows even the most common person to be able to view how relatable her life is to anyone else's. There is no smoke and mirrors or gimmicks; just a woman of God trying to get people to understand that there should never be excuses made when it comes to God. If He did not give excuses to the people, then why should we make any for ourselves?

Lorraine also looks at what it actually means to be single. It certainly does not mean to mingle like so many of us in the world would like to think or partake of. How about reading a story from someone who practices celibacy and faces the struggle of fighting temptation, when the flesh is tempted? What about the story of raising five children, practically alone, and having to care for herself and her children without looking for someone's assistance or handout? This story is a work soon to come. She makes it all happen by her sheer will and faith in the man above. Wait a minute! Did I just define solidified? Understand this is a test of faith and only the solidified have the ability to pass these daily tests. This lionesses' strength clearly shows that her faith is not waivered and after a few pages in, maybe you will start to question whether your faith would be tested.

Much of what is contained in the reading will force you to think. Knowing Lorraine, this is exactly what she wants you to do. So, if you find yourself questioning things in your life while you are reading this book, then welcome to her world. From her personal experiences, she wants you to understand that it is all right to be alone and when making these decisions it must be done wisely. She tells you why you DO NOT HAVE TO SETTLE. I had to write that in caps because so many people today are doing just that...SETTLING! As a result, divorce rates are at an all-time high, and marriages are ended on average before the two-year mark. YES, TWO YEARS! I am not making this up and why is this happening? Are these people in love or in lust? Are you married because your mate has "status"? Are you not married because you feel there are no good men or women still around?

Saved, Single, & Solidified in Christ

We have to understand people that not everyone is built for marriage, but some of us are. After reading chapters six through eight, it could very well provide you the knowledge to know if you are ready. For some that thought you were, maybe there is more work for you to do. The only way for any of you to find out is to read the book. Do not be the person at the book social that is lost from not getting this knowledge.

This work could only be created by someone who has lived these pains and struggles. I would advise anyone that does not feel this reading to go back and read again because I am telling you that you may have missed something. This work is possible only through the grace of God and if it were not for His grace then this foreword is pointless. This message is going to bless and strengthen someone; be it a friend, family member, neighbor, or co-worker.

I believe there is something in this book for everyone. Some of you will cry. Some may laugh. Others might just take notes because they are learning something. For those that do not take the time out to read, you are truly missing out on a treat. Lorraine is giving you this message because of her life, her struggle, and her pain. Dedication like this should only be rewarded and I promise to anyone that takes the time to read Saved, Single, and Solidified in Christ, you will not only be blessed, but have the opportunity to bless someone else. This powerful woman is only getting started. There will be more works and blessings to come through her writings.

Peace and Blessings
Delante A. Mouton, Jr.
Washington, D.C.
April, 2015

7

Introduction

The Bible says in Romans 10 verses 9 and 10, "⁹...if you confess with your mouth, "Jesus is Lord," and believe in your heart that God raised him from the dead, you will be saved. ¹⁰ For it is with your heart that you believe and are justified, and it is with your mouth that you confess and are saved. Being saved and single can sometimes be a little harder than it appears. However, it is a journey that you do not have to endure alone.

The word single according to Merriam-Webster's dictionary is defined as: "not having or including another; only one". It is also defined as: "not married or not having a serious romantic relationship with someone". Whether you are a widow, divorced, or simply had a broken relationship; the world categorizes you as single. Being saved and single allows us to defy all or at least part of these definitions.

The word solidify means to make or become hard or solid, make stronger; reinforce. Our salvation is the start of a journey to be a new person in Christ. Therefore, unlike the definition provided by Merriam-Webster's dictionary, when you are Saved, Single, and Solidified in Christ Jesus. We are not alone because His Holy Spirit is present in us to help us through the journey. You are romantically involved with God. You are in an exclusive relationship with your first love; that should be filled with intimacy, passion, joy, peace and above all pure unadulterated love!

If you are reading this book, it must be because you can identify with being saved, being single, or being in Christ. Maybe you can identify with one of these concepts or all three. Whatever the reason you have chosen to pick up this book I hope it helps you to grow in understanding and find peace in your journey as a single person.

Chapter 1
Thanks to the Christ in Me

Philippians 2:5
"Let this mind be in you which was also in Christ Jesus"

I am Lorraine Hopkins, the author of this text. I have written these pages because I know the struggles of being single, saved, and in Christ. When I first accepted the gift of salvation, it was in an exceptionally large local assembly that cared more about me learning to speak in tongues than me actually living right. I was a sixteen-year-old mother, who grew up in church. The years I spent in church I had no relationship with God, it was something I continued when I left home on my own as a matter of form, fashion, and routine.

I had a void and a life that was going downhill quickly. There was no one in the church that I could discuss my desires or the struggles of my flesh with, so I became a fornicator in the church. I clung to every word of the pastors and teachers because I lacked a true understanding of the scriptures. Reading the King James Version of the Bible was all I knew and frankly I could not make heads or tails of much of what it was saying.

I convinced myself based on the sermons that I would hear in the churches I attended that I could just keep willfully sinning and repenting and keep my salvation, without changing my heart intentions. As long as I asked for forgiveness, even though nothing was different in me - I was going to go home and do the same thing in a few hours - I was covered. I even had one Pastor tell me it was all right because I was basically like Paul in the Bible in

Romans 7:15-20, *"For what I am doing, I do not understand. For what I will to do, that I do not practice; but what I hate, that I do. 16 If then, I do what I will not to do, I agree with the law that it is good. 17 But now, it is no longer I who do it, but sin that dwells in me. 18 For I know that in me (that is, in my flesh) nothing good dwells; for to will is present with me, but how to perform what is good I do not find. 19 For the good that I will to do, I do not do; but the evil I will not to do, that I practice. 20 Now if I do what I will not to do, it is no longer I who do it, but sin that dwells in me."*

However, that Pastor could not have been more wrong. I was not like Paul. I enjoyed my sin. I enjoyed fornicating with my boyfriend. I

11

felt I would get a pass because we were in love, but there was one problem; he and I were not married. Eventually we became engaged, but would never arrive at the place of marriage, so I spent years giving that man something that did not belong to him, and I was all right with it.

The relationship ended on poor terms. I was left distraught. I was depressed, suicidal and felt I could not live without him. All this happened because I made him my God. You see I was having an affair with Jesus but giving my all to this man. I praised him for the way he touched me in bed, and I worshipped him for the way he made me feel as a woman. All the time I had a void that I thought he was filling with his false love, affections, and things. Therefore, when he left me, I almost lost my mind. The enemy had a trap set, but God had a different plan. You see I was saved because I had confessed with my mouth and believed in my heart that Christ died and rose from the grave (Romans 10:9-10).

I thought what he was giving me, doing to me, causing me to feel, was love. I believed these things because I was still conformed to the world. I had not truly experienced Christ. I did not allow the mind of Christ to be who I was. I was playing church. I would show up, worship (falsely), and leave feeling the same way I did when I walked in. I would have sex with this man and not realize that the high was limited and temporary and only lasted as long as we were being physical, not realizing once the touch of his hand was absent, so was my connection to him. I was lost. I did not realize that I had truly no knowledge of love. I did not realize that I had deep rooted issues which transpired back to my youth that left me vulnerable to the deception of the enemy.

Then suddenly it happened. All those messages that I heard as a child; those seeds that had been planted into my subconscious, began to play out in my mind. Somewhere along the journey, I met Christ for real and for myself. At that moment I realized I was living foul. I was not holy. I was looking for something to fill a void, which only God could. Just like me, you probably have had a similar, if not the same epiphany.

The point I am trying to make is I got there and so will you. I did not get there on my own. I arrived when I truly surrendered all that I am to Him. I began to work on my relationship with Him. I began to study His word. I started attending Bible study classes that allowed me to ask questions. I had a notebook to take notes. Instead of wasting my time watching meaningless shows on television, I began watching different preachers and teachers so I could get a basic understanding of some things. I even took notes on those programs. I questioned everything they said. My mind opened. I began to study everything I could because I wanted to know who He was and, in the process, I learned who we were to each other.

Several scriptures and definitions have been repeated throughout this text because they are important and serve as reminders to you. They are relevant at different points throughout the reading, as it will be in life. Therefore, the more familiar you become with His word the easier it will be to speak life to your situations.

I went through every step shared in each chapter of this text and then some that will be shared in my next work. The journey has not been peaches and cream every day of my life, but it has gotten easier, as I continue to grow in the knowledge of God's word and the power of the Holy Spirit. The joy of the Lord has truly become my strength. I am going to leave you with some tips in the closing chapter, which helped me to avoid temptation in my single status, so that you too may feel accomplished in being Saved, Single, and Solidified in Christ.

Chapter 2
Salvation to Born Again Single

II Corinthians 5:17 (NKJV)
"Therefore, if anyone is in Christ, he is a new creation;
old things have passed away; behold, all things have
become new."

Prior to accepting Jesus Christ in your life, you may have experienced a relationship or relationships that ended suddenly leaving you vulnerable, hurt, bruised, and/or confused. These relationships possibly left you broken and seeking something new to fill the void of that which once was. Perhaps you are single and have yet to experience a relationship but want to gain a deeper understanding of what your walk should look like. No matter the situation, this book can help you.

This chapter's opening scripture reminds us that when you accept Jesus Christ, you come into relationship with Him; hence if anyone is "in Christ", He is a new creature. You begin to walk in agreement with His word and believe that which is written in the word of God, to help you completely enter into your newness. Those old things that thought they would break you or prevent you from reaching success or your destiny are no longer relevant, except as a reminder of how far God has brought you.

When you go from being in a relationship to being single you have to change your mindset. Going from being in a relationship and unsaved to single and saved is an even greater transition. In some cases, you may be saved and, in a relationship, but carrying on as if you are not required to live holy. In these instances, your body or your flesh; in other words, has become accustomed to being in an intimate setting. It has become accustomed to affection, such as hugs and kisses. Many times, the body has experienced pre-marital sex, which caused feelings to be awakened and the flesh continues to desire that physical contact, although it is not appropriate outside of the sanctity of marriage. For these reasons, a reset button has to be pressed as it relates to your mind and how you think.

The Bible tells us in 1 Corinthians 7 verses 32 - 35, *"I want you to be free from anxieties. The unmarried man is anxious about the things of the Lord, how to please the Lord. But the married man is anxious about worldly things, how to please his wife and his interests are divided. And the unmarried or betrothed woman is anxious about the things of the Lord, how to be holy in body and spirit. But the married woman is anxious about worldly things, how to please her husband. I say this for your own benefit, not to lay any restraint upon you, but to promote good order and to secure your undivided devotion to the Lord."*

These scriptures reveal that as a single person, your number one priority is pleasing the Lord, whether male or female. It further states that you should be holy in your body and in your spirit. In order to be holy in body and spirit, you must first be holy in your mind and thinking. Therefore, you must enter into a process to help you bring your flesh subject, so that you can overcome those thoughts that ultimately became desires and feelings you once knew that can produce or result in sin.

You must guard what you put in your spirit; if you are trying to turn off the switch to past behaviors and change the way you think. There is a poem out there and the author is unknown, but I shared it below and it reads as follows:

By Changing Your Thinking
Unknown Author
By changing your thinking, you change your beliefs
When you change your beliefs, you change your expectations
When you change your expectations, you change your attitude
When you change your attitude, you change your behavior
When you change your behavior, you change your performance
When you change your performance, you change your life!!

You have to first recognize that reverting back to a single person from being in a relationship is a process. There are some things that have to take place and in every case some level of healing is required. Therefore, you must relieve yourself of any baggage that you are carrying from your ended relationship(s).

Nuggets may have been planted through harsh words that may have lowered your self-esteem. Maybe infidelity took place, and the trust was broken, now as a result of this you feel it impossible to believe a person can be truthful and faithful to you. Perhaps the person had an emotional affair, leaving you to feel neglected or without affection. It could simply be that you and the other person just realized you were not right for each other for whatever reason, and you parted on good terms, but this is still someone you had a connection with. Therefore, you felt rejected. Even the harshest reality may have taken place and your significant other may have passed away. No matter how the relationship came to an end; it ended, and you are single again.

Your reality right now is there is no one else, but you and God (if you're saved) or just you (if you are not). So how do you embrace being a born-again believer and not jeopardizing your salvation because you are single? How do you overcome the fear and trepidation that you feel when faced with the reality of being without a companion? You know that the process will not be easy, but a necessity to ensure that you are prepared to receive the mate God is preparing for you and sending your way. Even if you desire to remain single and live your life for Christ; that is all right too, but you still have to be healed to fulfill your purpose.

Isaiah 41:10 reads, *"Fear not, for I am with you; be not dismayed, for I am your God; I will strengthen you, I will help you, I will uphold you with my righteous right hand."*

Being saved and single puts you at an advantage over the unsaved single person because the Bible declares you have HELP! Yes, God not only declares that He is with you, but that He will strengthen you as well. The unsaved single person, in the eyes of the world, is alone; you are not. You have the assistance of the almighty to walk with you through the pruning process. Being saved and single means that the Christ in you is at work and you have the power you need to succeed on the journey.

Renewing your mind is never easy because old habits do indeed die hard. It is not easy to undo something that you have been doing for weeks, months, and possibly even years. Releasing feelings and desires that have been a normal part of your routine is necessary, but also a challenge. Simplicity and creativity become your friend in the process of renewing your mind.

The simplest way to renew your mind is to adhere to and apply the word of God. To be able to adhere to the word of God, you have to study it. Studying the word opens your mind to a deeper level of understanding as to what God wants and expects from us. Adhering to the word of God and being obedient gives direction on how to be successful. Everything you achieve in life, even being successful as a single person is associated with your faith. How then do you increase your faith enough to believe that you can accomplish that which you have set out to do? Romans 10:17 answers that question; *"faith comes by hearing and hearing the word of God."*

How can you hear the word unless you study it? The simple concept the word of God gives to help in the process of renewing your mind is found in Philippians 4 verses 8 and 9; which reads, *"8 Finally, brethren, whatever things are true, whatever things are noble, whatever things are just, whatever things are pure, whatever things are lovely, whatever things are of good report, if there is any virtue and if there is anything praiseworthy—meditate on these things. 9 The things which you learned and received and heard and saw in me, these do, and the God of peace will be with you."*

Meditation is what the Bible has instructed us to do. Meditation is a synonym for thinking. The Bible is telling us to focus our mind on extremely specific types of things. He is telling us to have pure thoughts. He is telling us to think about things that are lovely and are of good report. Notice the word does not tell us to focus on what the world is doing or believes to be good, but the things you should have learned, heard, received, and saw in Jesus Christ.

Realistically you can meditate on anything pure or impure, but the nature of your thoughts dictates your actions, which is why I shared the poem with you earlier in the book. There is truth in the poem. If you change your thinking, it will change your beliefs. Clearly if you are meditating on the word of God, it will change your beliefs.

Once you begin to believe the word of God, your expectations from God will ultimately reflect in your daily walk or lifestyle. Once those expectations change, you begin to develop a new and improved attitude of victory. Then your behavior changes because faith is ignited and you know who you are and whose you are; therefore, your life now changes to become pleasing to God.

Your walk is now a reflection of Christ. Before you know it; you have arrived! You have become that new creature that the Bible speaks about. Those old things that kept you in bondage; old mindsets, actions, deeds, and thought processes left you and have passed away, like the Bible declares. Everything about you has become new and your life has forever changed!

Chapter 3
Becoming A Renewed Virgin

Revelation 14:4
"It is these who have not defiled themselves with women, for they are virgins. It is these who follow the Lamb wherever he goes. These have been redeemed from mankind as first fruits for God and the Lamb..."

The biggest challenge to being single after being in a sexual relationship is abstaining. That is correct; you must become like a virgin all over again. Someone is saying, "I am reading this, I hear you," but I am not sure if I can do that one. Let me just reassure you that you can do it, because I have done it and am doing it! Acts 10:34 and Romans 2:11 both clearly confirm that we serve a God that is no respecter of persons, which means if you fear the Lord and live righteously, He can do the same thing for you that He has done for me.

The enemy does not want you to be successful at becoming a renewed virgin. He wants to redirect your thoughts to fleshly things. He wants you to stay connected to the old you, rather than embrace the new creature that you have become in Christ. He wants you to skip a day in the process of renewing your mind. He would like for you to meditate on those moments that you felt his or her touch or the negative words that were spoken into your spirit, so that those lies can resonate in your mind and become your reality. Yet, God wants you to be free of it, repented in our hearts, freed of guilt and condemnation in our minds and living a life filled with purpose orchestrated to glorify Him.

The Bible tells us in John 10:10, what the enemy is up to. It tells us what he has come to do. The scripture reads, *10 "the thief does not come except to steal, and to kill, and to destroy. I have come that they may have life, and that they may have it more abundantly."*

God wants you to LIVE the life He has purposed for you. The enemy must do everything in his power to stop you from succeeding. When we look at the world at large, at every turn the presence of sin or temptation is evident. You can actively see the works of the flesh at play in the music, from the song lyrics to the accompanying videos on the television, in the school systems and even in your local shopping areas. No person is exempt from being exposed to sin. The Bible even foretells that it shall be so in 1 John

2:16, which reads: *"16 For all that is in the world—the lust of the flesh, the lust of the eyes, and the pride of life—is not of the Father but is of the world."*

In all fairness, are you really expected to become a virgin again with all this going on around you? The answer is simple, yes! This is why; renewing the mind by meditating on those things which are pure is so crucial to your life. Honestly speaking, sometimes that will not be enough. You will have to go deeper into your spiritual arsenal than you have ever gone before; realizing that the weapons of our warfare are not carnal, but mighty to the pulling down of strong holds (1 Corinthians 10:4).

Feelings of loneliness, a desire to fornicate, thoughts of suicide, and depression are all strongholds that can come as a result of a broken relationship. These strongholds are what the enemy will try to use to steal your ability to practice abstinence. He will try to lower your self-esteem so that you feel undesirable. The remarkable thing about being "in Christ", is He provides you with weapons that give you the power and authority to cast down imaginations of every high thing that would try to exalt itself against the knowledge of God. He allows you to bring every thought into captivity and submit yourself in obedience to Christ (1 Corinthians 10:5), making it possible for you to truly become a virgin again.

You are probably asking yourself what does she mean to become a renewed virgin? I am sure you are thinking this is not even possible, because what is done cannot be undone. You are right. You can never get that first moment back, whether it was stolen from you against your will, or you released it voluntarily or prematurely; it happened, it is done, and it is over with. What you can do, if necessary, (because there are some who did things the right way), is repent and begin again.

If you did not do things as God intended you to, the first step is to acknowledge the sin, confess it before Him in prayer and ask His forgiveness. Once you have done that forgive yourself and move forward. Micah 7:19 tells us He will have compassion on us and cast our sin in the depths of the sea. Psalm 103:12 says, *"He removes our transgressions from us as far as the east is from the west."* Accept His forgiveness and hold on to the grace that He has so mercifully given, despite your past sin.

Do not allow your mind to be idle while trying to become a virgin again. One of the easiest ways to revert to past behaviors is having too much wasted time on your calendar. When you have time to waste, the enemy has time to try to infiltrate your thoughts. You must also be mindful of what you are filling your time with. That means if you are reading trashy sex novels; stop it now! If you are watching television shows filled with lustful acts of fornication or other sexually immoral acts; change the channel! If you have a playlist that you used to listen to when you were lost in sin; delete it.

These things will tug at your heart, having your thoughts going back to a place you have been freed from. The Bible tells us that *"the heart is deceitful above all things, and desperately wicked, who can know it"* (Jeremiah 17:9). In addition, Proverbs 4:23 reads: *"Keep your heart with all diligence, for out of it springs the issues of life."*

To prevent the enemy from stealing what God has given us upon becoming born again; we must guard our thoughts and our hearts because the two can lead us astray if we are not careful. Being proactive and taking steps to manage your time and guard what you allow to enter your vessel can help you tremendously with remaining abstinent. Establish both short- and long-term goals for yourself. Once you have done so, actively work towards them.

Develop a routine. For me personally, my routine requires me to be so vigorous that by the end of the day, all I want to do is rest. When you are just beginning the process of abstaining from sexual activity, it may be best to organize your day to minimize down time until you are able to demonstrate self-control in those areas of struggle.

By setting goals you are giving yourself something to focus on, other than the flesh and its desires. This is a healthy way to accomplish some things in your life, for God's purpose or for your personal growth and development. Allow yourself to live a life filled with purpose. When you remove the distractions, such as programs that are inappropriate on television and other ungodly and unholy hindrances, something happens. You now have time to focus. You have time to do things that will make you productive. Your mind unfolds to levels it has not experienced, probably in a long time, because of everything else that was a priority that should not have been. Use this time to increase your study time, prayer life, and fasting. Take this opportunity to give God your best. This is also a fantastic opportunity to focus on health and wellness.

Maybe you have had a desire to lose weight, or you always wanted to learn to play an instrument; this is the time to fulfill some of those positive goals. This is a time when you can consecrate yourself and improve your relationship with the Father. This is the time that you can work on yourself. You can take some classes, do some volunteer work in your community or mentor someone. This is the time when you should be discovering your God given purpose and allowing that which He has planted in your belly to be birthed and come to life. You have no distractions; therefore, you have no excuse.

Becoming a virgin again can be the best thing ever if you allow it to be. If you keep your mind focused on the things of God, He will take you places you did not know you could go. Matthew 6:33 tells us, *"Seek yeah first the kingdom of God and all of His righteousness and everything else shall be added unto you."*

Although the journey will place you in situations of challenge, you must have the mind of Christ if you have any chance of overcoming. I encourage you to live out Philippians 2:5 and do as it says, *" Let this mind be in you which was also in Christ Jesus."*

Chapter 4
Cannot Control the Desire

1 Corinthians 7:9
"But if they cannot exercise self-control, let them marry. For it is better to marry than to burn with passion."

Galatians 5 verses 22 and 23 reads, *"But the fruit of the spirit is love, joy, peace, forbearance, kindness, goodness, faithfulness, gentleness, and self-control. Against such things there is no law."*

This is a familiar passage of scripture and the church, as well as believers often speak on many of these topics. Those most often referenced and are probably most common to us all are love, joy, peace, kindness, goodness, faithfulness, and gentleness. Very rarely do you hear anyone mention when paraphrasing these passages of scripture forbearance. The other fruit that is rarely mentioned, often overlooked, and least spoken about in my opinion is self-control.

Often, I wondered why that is. Is it because we as people feel that we are in control, as long as we are not committing offenses that are acceptable to the world? Prime example, engaging in fornication is not seen as lacking self-control in our supposedly "Christian", but truly carnal mindset, as long as we have one partner and are in love. The devil is a liar! If this is what you are telling yourself to help you sleep better at night and continue in your sin it is time to repent. This is the mindset of a lukewarm or double minded person. If you believe it is acceptable to be saved and sin continuously and you are still protected by the grace of God, you are wrong!

Hebrews 10 verses 26 and 27 read: *"26 If we deliberately keep on sinning after we have received the knowledge of the truth, no sacrifice for sins is left, 27 but only a fearful expectation of judgment and of raging fire that will consume the enemies of God."*

That means you have to obey, 1 Peter 1:16 reads, *"16 for it is written: "Be holy, because I am holy."*

As a born-again believer you cannot enter into the light, be exposed to the truth, and knowingly wallow in the same filth and expect to keep your salvation. At this point you are taking advantage of the grace of God and placing yourself on the chopping block to receive an eternal resting place in hell. None of us who have received and believe in Christ as our Lord and Savior want to experience this. We want to hear God say, "well done my good and faithful servant," not, "get thee away from me for I never knew you who practiced evil" (Matthew 7:23).

God is not pleased with double minded Saints. He is not pleased with lukewarm believers. It is evident in His word. God says to the lukewarm Christian in Revelations 3 verses 15 and 16, *"I know your works, that you are neither cold nor hot. I could wish you were cold or hot. 16 so then, because you are lukewarm, and neither cold nor hot, I will vomit you out of My mouth."*

The word is talking about puking people up! That means something about lukewarm people has upset God to the point He has decided to reject them by way of vomit. Regurgitation is a form of purging toxic fluid planted on the inside of you that your body is not accustomed to. Therefore, your body will reject and discard it as waste. This is a direct correlation of how God views the lukewarm Christian. He rejects what is not in accordance with His will. He prefers that you make a decision and pick a side. Choose to be either cold or hot (sinner or saved), because being in the middle, neutral, or undecided is not benefiting your cause to reach the Kingdom of God.

The Bible declares that *"the double minded man is unstable in all his ways"*, (James 1:8). This is not pleasing to the Lord, because such a person lives in a constant state of compromise. Typically, the double-minded believer lives a double life. This is the type of person you really do not know, because in their mind they are living for the world and Christ at the same time. However, you should know that light and darkness cannot exist in the same space. Eventually one will corrupt the other. The Bible is clear, *"No one can serve two masters; for either he will hate the one and love the other, or else he will be loyal to the one and despise the other. You cannot serve God and mammon,"* (Matthew 6:24).

If you do not know what mammon is, it is defined as material wealth or possessions; especially as having a debasing influence. Double minded Christians are typically fans of Christ but have not embraced the process of renewing their minds. They have not achieved the state of being selfless and fully surrendered to God. Therefore, there is a struggle with releasing old habits. Due to the failure to renew the mind, the believer has now been placed in a situation where they are distracted by carnal things that eventually manifest into actions, which becomes sin.

There is a battle going on within that is causing the believer to disobey and make excuses. They have been convinced that their behaviors are acceptable; however, in the eyes of God that is not the case. Although, the intent is to walk with the Lord, double minded behaviors and acting out your own free will circumvents the Holy Spirit's ability to use you the way you were commissioned or called to be used, because your heart and mind have not been fully surrendered to God. God, in the meantime, is waiting for a real YES or a real NO from His people.

God does not desire false witnesses. He wants believers who will worship Him in spirit and in truth (John 4:23), but there is no truth in a double life. A double life and lukewarm living are living a lie. I tried it personally and failed terribly. It was not until I gave God a real YES, that I began to win in this race!

Surrendering the heart and mind to God is essential to your success as a single individual. In order to be single, saved, and solidified in

Christ, you must be committed and disciplined. It is when you are in relationship with Christ that you are able to control those things that can come back and serve as a distraction or hinder you from thinking clearly when tempted. When you are in a natural relationship, your flesh has developed a routine and becomes accustomed to some things that you will need the power of the Holy Spirit to break! The power of the Holy Spirit is what helps you to become a creature of self-discipline. Your relationship with Christ is supernatural and filled with power!

In the relationship with Christ, you have to pray, fast, and study. This relationship is built on faith and love. *"Now faith comes by hearing and hearing the word of God"*, (Romans 10:17). Therefore, to maintain a healthy relationship with Christ, there has to be many intimate moments throughout the day with Him. In those moments, you will not only speak to Him, but He will speak to you also. Those moments are created in your study, prayer, and fasting time.

When a natural relationship ends; it is never easy, whether you departed amicably or under hostile conditions. You will need to reveal the fruit of self-discipline and do so expeditiously. If there were any sexual relations involved, it becomes even more difficult to sever that bond. Many attempt to find ways to abstain from sexual activities until marriage, but oftentimes still wrestle with the spirit(s) of perversion they attached themselves to when they engaged in premarital relations. If those thoughts are not purged, the mind is deceived into returning to immoral sexual acts, which can lead to problems.

Single people who consider themselves saved are now in a compromising position where they desire to fulfill the lust of the flesh; although they know it is wrong. Since they lack much needed self-control, they disobey God and participate in acts of fornication or other sexually immoral activities to gratify the flesh and its desires. With today's technology, individuals can engage in discreet meetings by connecting online from popular sites as common as Craig's List. Others will hire prostitutes and lay with them or engage in random sexual encounters with people they do not know, all to please the flesh.

1 Corinthians 6:16 says, *"Or do you not know that he who is joined to a prostitute becomes one body with her? For, as it is written, "The two will become one flesh."*

This scripture makes it clear that when we partake in sexual acts with another person, we are joining ourselves to them, becoming one. Why would you join yourself to a harlot or a prostitute? Why do you believe that you are still covered by the grace of God when you are willingly engaging in sin, despite knowing the truth? Many believe that their salvation is infinite. You cannot knowingly and willfully sin against God and still be covered by His grace after learning the truth. Hebrews 10:26 confirms this for us. Again, it reads: *"For if we sin willfully after we have received the knowledge of the truth, there no longer remains the sacrifice for sins..."*

With that being said, many need to repent for their disobedience and make every effort to become a renewed virgin or to marry as the scripture tells us. Making a mistake is one thing but repeating the same mistake over and over is a choice. It would be better to marry than to burn with passion or to have to answer to God in judgment, because you could not control your fleshly desires. 1 Corinthians 7:2 even tells us, *"Nevertheless, because of sexual immorality, let each man have his own wife, and let each woman have her own husband."*

This is yet another example of the word of God encouraging marriage over sexual immorality. If you cannot control your flesh, wait on the good husband or great wife that God has ordained for you. Sex outside of marriage can yield disastrous results. When one exposes themselves to prostitutes, harlots, or random partners harsh realities become possibilities in your life. Diseases: such as HIV, AIDS, the new super strand of gonorrhea, warts in the genital area and even pregnancy can occur and interrupt and delay your destiny.

While marriage is one option, when your behavior exhibits that which is contrary to the word, there are several resources to try to bring the flesh subject. Some spirits encountered can quite possibly be more than you can handle in the flesh. Therefore, if you are caught not wearing the whole armor of God, as instructed, and find yourself caught in a vulnerable moment; the enemy can penetrate the fortress that should have been protected. Now a foothold has been given to the enemy and he is trying to break you with a powerful addiction in the flesh.

I am not saying that you will be perfect, but you should be striving towards mirroring Christ in your day-to-day life. You should make every effort to live a righteous life. Will you make mistakes; always. However, you need to recognize the difference in a decision to willfully sin against God's commandments versus an error in judgment.

Making a conscious decision, when you know better, to do the wrong thing is not a mistake; it is a choice. A mistake is unintentional, unplanned, not premeditated. To make the same "mistake" repeatedly, without any conviction or effort to change is a choice. Choose to try every day to release sinful behavior and live a Christ like life and if you fall; repent quickly, with a pure heart. Do not conform to sin, change. God judges the heart of a man, not his actions. If your heart is not set on living holy, God knows. He knows everything, even the things man cannot see.

Chapter 5
Use Your Weapons

2 Corinthians 10: 4-6
⁴ "For the weapons of our warfare are not carnal but mighty in God for pulling down strongholds, ⁵ casting down arguments and every high thing that exalts itself against the knowledge of God, bringing every thought into captivity to the obedience of Christ, ⁶ and being ready to punish all disobedience when your obedience is fulfilled."

I cannot pretend that being single is a cakewalk. It is not. Naturally, if you have ever been in a relationship, you will desire companionship. Going from a relationship to single will come with a certain level of temptation, but the Bible says in 1 Corinthians 10 verse 13: *"No temptation has overtaken you except such as is common to man; but God is faithful, who will not allow you to be tempted beyond what you are able, but with the temptation will also make the way of escape, that you may be able to bear it."*

The wonderful thing about God is He helps the helpless. When you read His word, you realize the mercies of our God. He knew what obstacles would be faced before you or I ever did. He even confirmed in His word that we will be tempted and being the magnificent God that He is, He promises you will not be tempted beyond what you are able to handle. He does not stop there. He even provides you with a promise of help; should an issue present itself. He said if you do become tempted, He will provide a way of escape so that you are able to handle it and not submit to sin. If that is not merciful, I do not know what is. That is the kind of God you and I serve. We serve a God who wants to see us successful!

God also equips you for the fight. He gave you weapons to use in times of trouble. He prepared you for the warfare. He knew what would come your way. It is human nature to sin. David qualifies it in Psalm 51:5, when he reminds us that *he was brought forth in iniquity and in sin did his mother conceive him.* Were we not born under the same conditions?

To gain control over your flesh and your sin comes with a process. Sin comes because of temptation to the flesh. Therefore, you must acknowledge what your weaknesses are. In what areas am I struggling? Ask yourself, why am I weak as it relates to temptation?

Each person has their own temptation or area of struggle. Even Jesus was tempted, although He never sinned. You can study it in Hebrews 4:15. Typically, along with the struggle of temptation comes deficiencies within your personality, because of life experiences.

You may crave attention because you were neglected. You may be insecure because of unhealthy past relationships. You may not understand your worth because no one ever told you how valuable you are. In most instances you succumb to your temptation because of brokenness, lack of healing, or the yearning for acceptance. There is usually someone or something that has caused you pain and as a result one responds with sin.

There is also the person who is irresponsible and simply enjoys doing wrong things. There too underlies a root cause to their behaviors. No matter the issue, no matter the cause, the first step is admitting who you are and acknowledging your struggle within. You must face it, whatever area it is, and confess it.

Confession is one of the weapons God has given us to overcome the plan of the enemy. The enemy cannot hold anything against you that you are not hiding. It is the secret sins that he uses to expose you and destroy you from the inside out.

The Bible tells us in James 5:16, *to confess our sins to each other and pray for each other that we may be healed.* It is important that you are transparent in this walk with God. You have to be able to admit where you fall short, so that others may pray with you and for your situation, because PRAYER does change THINGS!

Each of us face different temptation(s), but you are not the only one who has had to face your issue. There is someone out there who has dealt with something similar to your situation, if not the exact same thing. Someone has been delivered from your situation just so that they could help you to overcome it. *"We all overcome by the blood of the Lamb and the word of their testimony"*, (Revelation 12:11).

There are people who God has allowed to go through the struggle before you, in order for them to confirm for you it is possible for you to do the same or even greater. How can you receive your help, if you are in denial about your struggle, or refuse to be open and honest about what you are facing? Transparency is necessary.

Another weapon at your disposal is prayer. There will be temptations that you deal with that may seem to be more than you can handle. You might feel that it is going to get the best of you, but again you have the power. You have been equipped with everything you need to succeed at overcoming that obstacle that is trying to cause you to fall.

The reason you feel the temptation is more than you can handle is because you do not believe in the power that lives within you. Luke 10:19 says, *"the Father has given us authority to overcome the power of the enemy and nothing will harm us,"* but you still do not believe that you are the primary authoritative figure in your circumstance.

When the temptation you face appears to be a huge mountain in your path that you cannot see your way around; pray! If you feel the prayers are not helping or working quickly enough for you, then you may have to incorporate another weapon we do not use as often as we should, and that is fasting.

Matthew 17:20-22 talks about our ability to say to the mountains in our lives move from here to there and they will move. The scripture further explains that nothing will be impossible for you. However, you cannot accomplish this type of result without prayer and fasting. You see this scripture also recognizes the lack of faith in a person, as Jesus mentions things are not happening because of unbelief. He explains that if you can just have mustard seed faith, this is the kind of power you can possess.

Your mouth is a weapon in this battle. Proverbs 18:21, teaches us *"the tongue has the power of life and death and those who love it will eat its fruit."* What this means is that everything we speak either brings about life to a situation or death to it. For example, if you are struggling with your flesh and you speak out of your mouth, "I cannot control myself"; you have just killed your ability to take control over your situation.

Look at it another way. If I am struggling in my flesh, but I say it shall not have control over me because I am going too fast and pray that this flesh will come subject to the power of the Holy Spirit that lives within me and I believe that in my heart and my mind; I have just spoken life and declared the victory over my situation. We simply need to learn to reframe our way of thinking to align with God's word.

It would be the same result if you were sick in your body. Your words have the power to condemn you to the grave or resurrect you from the dead. Jesus is the resurrection, and the life, and we who believe in Him live, even though one day this flesh will surely die (John 11:25). If you are going to walk around sick in your body and say things like, "I cannot handle this illness, I could go any day now", you have just spoken yourself into the grave and demonstrated that you have no faith in God or the power He has given you!

Faith and doubt cannot dwell in the same space because a positive coupled with a negative cancel each other out. You have killed your hope. If the Bible says in Mark 5:34, "thy faith has made the whole," why then would you speak yourself into the grave or prolonged illness? Rather, take your words and say to that illness, "I bind you up. I cast you out of my body; by my faith in Jesus' ability to heal me - I am healed." If you declare and decree in the name of Jesus that you will live and not die, then you are speaking life to your situation and prophesying to yourself. If your faith is aligned with your tongue, then you shall reap the fruit of what you have spoken.

Please understand my statement regarding the importance of speaking life and exercising faith. If your faith is aligned with your thoughts and words, you will reap that which you speak and believe. Many speak of death and die because they already believe they have lost the battle, while others speak life and live because they already believe they have the victory, they live. It is up to you to choose because again, you have the power. God has already given it to you. Study Isaiah 38:1-7; 2 Kings 20:1-11

Neither man nor woman are exempt from temptation. At the end of the day, it is when we do not acknowledge and deal with the temptation that comes our way, that it will manifest itself and become sin. When you are single you are equipped to win and overcome the temptation that presents itself before you. Use your tools because you cannot lose with the power you have in the Holy Spirit.

Chapter 6
It Is Okay to Be Alone

Hosea 2:19-20
" I will betroth you to me forever.
I will betroth you in righteousness and justice,
in love and compassion.
I will betroth you in faithfulness,
and you will acknowledge the LORD."

Everyone was not designed to be with another person. There are many people who have mastered the art of being alone. There is nothing wrong with making a decision to dedicate your life, time, and your talents to the Lord. In Hosea God says, He will marry you to Himself forever. He will marry you in righteousness, justice, love, and compassion. He will do so in faithfulness, and you will know that He is Lord of your life. That is a promise and a marriage bond that cannot be broken, because the God we serve is not like man that He should lie. Whatever He says, He will do it (Numbers 23:19). Whatever He speaks from His mouth cannot return to Him void (Isaiah 55:11).

Being married to God is the safest, most fulfilling, relationship any person can enter. When you are single, the Lord should be your primary focus. The Bible mentions a desire that all men should remain single (1 Corinthians 7:7), but it was understood that we were not all designed the same. It is clear in the word that each person has been given their own gifting from God.

1 Corinthians 7:8 reads, *but I say to the unmarried and to widows that it is good for them if they remain even as I;* meaning single. Therefore, if you possess the ability to abstain from a relationship, it is preferred that you do. Paul recognizes that the single person has more time to devote to the Lord.

Ephesians 5 talks about how the church is the bride of Christ, which means you, because the church is not a building. The church is the body of believers who live and follow Christ. Although the Bible spends a great deal of time outlining marriage, you have to understand that your relationship with Christ is the most important relationship you will ever encounter in this life.

The world often highlights the joys of sex as a reason to marry, but in reality, many of those joys are built on false expectation and a damaged mindset. Several single believers buy into this thought process because they face challenges in understanding their self-worth. The idea that you may have unfulfilled desires remaining in a single state has left many to believe that marriage is a necessity. Many leaders place an emphasis on marriage and highlight the benefits of it, in most instances connecting those benefits to the pleasures of being able to engage in a sexual relationship and companionship. However, marriage is work that extends far beyond sexual gratification.

When you summarize and limit the benefits of marriage to this, it is very superficial. A person who desires to remain single should not have such pressures thrust upon them or be left to feel inadequate for making a decision to live a single life to glorify the Lord. In many modern-day churches if you are single, you cannot hold certain positions, such as a Deacon or Pastor. This is sad because that would mean that Paul and our very own Lord and Savior Jesus Christ (our chief priest) would not be able to hold these offices within some local assemblies today.

Therefore, if you desire to be like Jesus Christ and the Apostle Paul and remain single and live a life to the glory of God, by all means do so. Do not allow anyone to belittle your decision or convince you that you should not live in such a manner. Do not allow the carnal thinking of man to place you in a stereotypical category. Just because many believe that people cannot live or function without companionship or the touch of another person, does not make it true.

God has gifted us each differently. Because others may not be able to maintain self-control, does not mean that is your reality. You are not valued less in the Kingdom of God because you are single. Always remember what God says, before walking in what man says, because as the word said; singleness is preferred!

Many will try to convince you that you will lack self-control. Others will tell you that you need support and companionship, in the form of a mate. Whatever their thought process is, you must perform God's will for you and know that you are able to do all things through Christ who strengthens you (Philippians 4:13).

You maintain your life of being single not in your own strength, but through the power of the Holy Spirit. If someone tries to discourage you or put you down, remember the thief comes only to steal, kill, and destroy. The thief comes in many forms. He may come disguised as a parent, preacher (hireling), teacher, or a friend. Since the word of God is true, you have all the power to withstand what comes your way!

If you live a single life, embrace it and be a living testimony to help others. The Bible clearly states that when a person is married, they are concerned with the things of the world and their focus is on how to please their spouse. However, you, the single person, are free of such concerns. Your concern is centered on the things of the Lord and how to please Him (1 Corinthians 7:32-34), unlike the married person who has divided interest.

Be proud of your choice and do not be ashamed to live a life for God as an example of who you are gifted and designed to be. Being single is not a sin and do not allow anyone to lead you to accept that it is. During this time draw near to God and identify with Jesus, who was the living example of how the single person should live life.

Chapter 7
Is Marriage for You?

Ephesians 5:31
"For this reason, a man shall leave his father and mother and be joined to his wife, and the two shall become one flesh."

In Chapter four we talked about not being able to control the desire. 1 Corinthians 7:9 reads, "*but if they cannot exercise self-control, let them marry. For it is better to marry than to burn with passion*", was the reference scripture for that chapter.

In this chapter I would like to elaborate on marriage. As discussed in the last chapter, marriage may not be for everyone, but clearly the Bible tells us it is for some. It is for those who burn with passion, it is for those who desire to have families, those who can see themselves becoming one flesh with another, among other reasons. Some marry because they are looking for love, while others desire to be loved. Whatever the reason, marriage is an institution not to be entered into lightly.

During your time as a single person, you should have learned and developed several qualities to prepare you to be an effective husband or wife. The relationship you have with Jesus Christ is simply a period of preparation to help establish you for your desired role. You are probably asking yourself, "How so?"

When you are single and born-again, you should be in a committed relationship with Jesus Christ. Remember in the earlier chapter we discussed that you are married to Him. In that relationship you live a life reflective of who He is. You are focused on loving others. You are faithful in spending time with Him. You understand intimacy because it should be something you now share regularly with the Lord. You have grasped the concept of being faithful and dedicated to one person. You understand what unconditional love looks like and now know how to reciprocate that love to another. Therefore, being saved, single, and solidified in Christ is so important. This is the time you use to learn yourself, be healed and advance in your thinking and gain an understanding of what a companion truly is.

Should you decide that marriage is for you, do not pursue marriage. If you pursue marriage, then love becomes subservient to it. If your focus is on getting married, then things like love and friendship become less important. Ultimately, you may find yourself in a situation you did not intend to be in. In a search for your soul mate, you may get caught up in superficial characteristics and distractions that may cause you to falsely conclude that you have found the one. This is why you have to ensure all the things you learned in your relationship with Jesus Christ, as a single person, remain at the forefront of your thinking. You need the principles you learned in your relationship with Christ to transcend your emotions.

For the duration of time you spend as a single person, you should allow yourself to be healed of past hurts and issues, to prevent bringing baggage into any relationship. It is highly recommended that while you are single you consecrate yourself. Constantly pray and ask God for His wisdom. You want Gods' wisdom first, to be sure you are doing what God wants; in deciding to marry. In addition, His wisdom will help you to make the right choice, because as Jeremiah 17:9 reads, *"the heart is deceitful above all things, and desperately wicked; who can know it?"*

It is a challenge trying to maintain the mind and heart of Christ within yourself, in an effort to please God. In addition, trying to understand another's heart is even more difficult. You are unable to clearly see the motives and intentions of another person if you are not praying and asking God for wisdom and the power to discern. The flesh will mislead you as well as the heart because they both desire what they desire. When the flesh or heart is tempted, the carnal mind (a mind not connected to Christ) will induce thoughts that will allow its desires to come to fruition.

Marriage may be the next step for you; after spending a healthy amount of time in relationship with Christ, as a single person. If that is the case, be cautious of the transition. It is not difficult to fall back into prior thinking and behaviors. Bring God into the transition, that you will not revert to former thinking and get more than you bargained for.

Chapter 8
Choose Wisely

Amos 3:3
"Can two walk together, unless they are agreed?"

When the Holy Spirit confirms in you that marriage is indeed for you, there is now a decision that has to be made. At some point you will be left to decide if the person before you is who God has intended for you. Therefore, do not leave this decision strictly to the heart, but invoke the power of discernment given by the Holy Spirit. Since God gives you free will, you have to choose wisely.

The opening scripture for this chapter asks a powerful question, "Can two walk together, unless they are agreed?" Ponder on that for a moment. Now ask yourself, can you catch a ride with someone going in a different direction than you and arrive at your destination? If you are headed to a specific place by bus, train, or airplane, you get directions as to the appropriate route to take so that you may arrive at the place you want to get to on time. If for any reason you board the wrong bus, plane, or train; one of two things is going to happen. Either you are going to be late arriving at your destination or you will not get there at all; if you do not correct the error you made on the journey.

As in the examples that I shared, choosing the wrong person to walk with in life, is the same as boarding the wrong bus, plane, or train. If that person has no desire to go where you are going or to support the things God has called you to, then you will find yourself in a situation where you lose you and cater to being who that person wants you to be in their life.

The Bible says in Genesis 2:18, *"then the Lord God said, "It is not good for man to be alone; I will make him a helper suitable for him."*

When God created woman, He did not design her to be anything to man other than a wife, mother, helper, and lifelong companion. If she was not a wife, she was to be used to the glory of God. Even with Mary we see this. She was a virgin who miraculously conceived Jesus, but God still gave her a husband as a covering for her life.

Mary's life had purpose. She was to bring forth the son of God, and God was careful to select a man who would heed the voice of the angel and help Mary to fulfill the purpose God predestined for her. God is no respecter of persons; therefore, God is not going to send you anyone to prevent you from completing the purpose He assigned to your life.

As we saw in Genesis God created Adam a helper. The word helper is defined as a person who assists someone. Looking at this from a biblical perspective, the helper is the support for the man. It also means to share in a task. The use of the word helper in the Hebrew context means that he is inadequate without her. Helper does not make the woman inferior, rather it defines the woman's role and position. Although the woman is the weaker vessel and a helper, it certainly does not depreciate her value.

Man was created in the image of God and the woman was created from man and for him that through God's perfect design the two would become one under the sanctity of marriage, as we read in Genesis 2:24 and Mark 10:8. God made man and woman to complement one another. They flow in unison and match each other's efforts. Where one is weak the other is strong and vice versa. When you become one flesh, you bring balance and wholeness to each other.

God created woman from the rib of the man. He removed a part of him to create her. Once a man connects with the right woman; it is as if he has found a missing piece of himself. Therefore, they flow in unison and the marriage has peace. Although they are two separate bodies, they are one with each other in spirit. They defy the odds and glorify God in their commitment and sacrifices made for one another's success. They win together.

God could have created woman out of any part of the man's anatomy, but He chose the rib. The rib is used to protect major organs within the body. It is often speculated that for this reason the man should protect his wife in a like manner. It is further believed that God chose the rib from his side for them to be equal and walk alongside one another throughout life. Finally, because the rib is close to the heart, He also should love her.

Although these statements are not actually biblical, it is a nice thought. However, there are some things in the word of God concerning marriage that we do know to be true. First, we know that a man that finds a wife finds a good thing and obtains favor from God (Proverbs 18:22). You know that the heart of a husband has confidence in his wife, and he lacks no gain. She brings him good and not evil all the days of her life (Proverbs 31:11-12). As we can see through all these different biblical references marriage is honorable and surely yields its own rewards.

While spending time as a single person in intimacy, fellowship, and relationship with the Lord, there are some things about yourself that you should have discovered. You should now know who you are to God and who you are in Christ, along with knowing for what purpose you were created. To make provision for the wrong person in your life can delay or divert your destiny. When it is time to choose, you have to choose wisely, because the thief has come to steal, kill, and destroy your purpose.

Prayers are heard by God and the enemy. The enemy will try to answer your prayer with a wolf and unless you are careful to discern if the response is from God or your flesh, you may welcome that wolf into your life. What happens when the wolf is embraced? Often it starts off as peaches and cream, wine, and roses, but in time it becomes a real-time, real-life nightmare. You will feel like you have awakened in a bad dream, because when the wolf came to you it appeared to be everything you asked for. What you did not realize was that person who came to you was wearing a costume all along.

If a person does not know the love of God, the likelihood of them understanding love and knowing how to love you unconditionally is slim to none. What you have to understand is the word of God teaches both the man and the woman what the expectations are concerning their relationship. It is clear that the man is to love his wife as Christ loved the church and be willing to lay down his life for her. He is also expected to be the head of the wife as Christ is the head of the church. A man is expected to sanctify his wife and cleanse her by washing of water by the word of God. A man is to love his wife in the same manner in which he loves his own body. A man who loves his wife, loves himself according to God's word.

Just as there are some major expectations and instructions for the male, there too are expectations and instructions for the female. As a woman you are to submit to your husband as to the Lord. Recall, I mentioned that your singleness, it is a time of preparation for those who desire to be married. In the time that you are or were single you should have been in a state of submission to the Lord, which equips you to be able to replicate this behavior in marriage. You, as a female, are expected to be unto your own husband in everything. Although the Bible does not tell the woman to love her husband, it does tell her to respect him. These concepts concerning the expectations of the male and female can be found in Ephesians 5:22-33.

To love another, to respect one another, to submit to another, and to care for someone the way that you would care for your own body requires a relationship with God. This kind of love is selfless and requires the mind of Christ (Philippians 2:5). The love between the married pair, the relationship, and the evolution from two separate beings to one flesh is described in the Bible as a mystery.

A carnal minded person cannot fathom such behaviors. A carnal mind is not capable of understanding this type of love. The nature or as the Bible says it, the deeds of the flesh are evident, and it does not look anything like that which Christ displays (Galatians 5:19). God is love. You cannot know, process, possess, or understand real love like this without knowing, understanding and being in relationship with

Him. Therefore, you must choose carefully. You must choose a person that understands, not only that God is love, but also respects and knows God's expectations and definition of love. No one is capable of giving something they do not understand or possess.

Chapter 9
Do Not Settle

2 Corinthians 6:14
"Do not be unequally yoked together with unbelievers. For what fellowship has righteousness with lawlessness? And what communion has light with darkness?"

While you may be considering transitioning from the path of a single person to a couple, remember the words of the previous chapter; choose wisely. In the selection process you will meet all sorts of characters and yes; I did mean characters. Therefore, you will truly need to call on the wisdom of God and discernment. You will have to exude patience in the process of discerning the spirits of others. If you are not patient, then your hunt for companionship may end sooner than you think.

Dating, or as I like to say courting, is a remarkably interesting process. It is an activity many devote a great deal of time to that in several instances, ultimately becomes wasted time, when reflected upon. I have encountered people who have been in a relationship with a person for three, five, eight, ten, sixteen and some even twenty plus years, who have no intention of marrying. Attempting to avoid being alone, these individuals held on to something that had no promise of a righteous future. They allowed themselves to settle for something God would not want for them. They made a decision not to trust God to give them greater or bring them to what they are truly deserving of.

Oftentimes, men and women meet someone and begin courting them in desperation, which is the wrong reason. There is something attractive about the other person: the way they look, how they make you smile, or how they make you feel good about you when you are with them. Something about them temporarily fills that void that you did not allow Jesus to touch, heal, and deliver you from.

When this happens you accept relationships that do not meet your standards and in due course you settle for something that you chose for yourself and coaxed yourself into believing was a gift from God. Yes, the companionship may temper the sting of loneliness, but in your heart of hearts, way deep down inside you know that you need to let this thing go. Why? Because it does not fulfill you spiritually, emotionally, or mentally. You may have physical needs being met, but you feel shame and guilt because you know in your truest form that God is not pleased with your actions to put your salvation on the shelf to have a man or woman in your life.

When you are a single person: SAVED, SINGLE, SOLIDIFIED in Christ, that means that you do not settle for anything less than what God wants for you. That means that when you realize on the first date that this person is not equally yoked with your beliefs or thoughts concerning life; the invitation for the second date should never be accepted or extended. Instead, what you do is look into those big doe eyes or get caught up in the charming words and before you realize it you have forgotten to ask the questions that really matter. Then you end up on additional dates that you should not have been on.

This grows into a form of a relationship, which is empty. Years go by and you realize you are in a relationship with someone you do not even know. You each have worn a mask to allow each other to see the absolute best in each other, with none of the negatives. Many single believers then fall into acts of fornication and settle for sex outside of marriage or in other words, sex without commitment. (Because you are not "married" it should not be) God wants you to have more than that. God wants you to have all that He predetermined for your life, but when you settle, you can sometimes delay your blessing.

When you settle you entertain the enemy. You give him a foothold into your life, and you cannot afford to do that as a born-again believer, because as Hebrews 10:26 tells us, *"For if we sin willingly after we have received the knowledge of the truth, there remains no more sacrifice for sins"*. In other words, you now know better, so you are supposed to do better. If you do not do what you know is right, you must repent quickly or be held accountable.

You see the first date is not actually a date; it is an interview. If they fail the interview the rejection letter should be sent immediately. If you find enough potential for a successful union, then the position may need to be granted on a temporary basis. If employers give a ninety-day trial, why should you not be willing to do the same. The trial for you may not last ninety days. What you did not discover in one date, you may be able to narrow down in a few more. What happens when you apply for a job? Do you get it after the first interview? Not most times. If you say or do something to spark the interest of the interviewer then in most cases, they bring you back for a second and sometimes even a third interview, before you are offered the position.

You have to be like an employer hiring a candidate for a position in their organization; after all, this is your life partner we are talking about. Employers have a job description with expectations for the candidate to be able to fulfill. That posting usually contains required and preferred skills. In the same manner you should have certain qualities and characteristics that you want in your mate. You should know your deal breakers versus your preferences. It is crucial that you make that distinction.

Naturally, you need to be realistic, and you should not expect them to be perfect, checking every box. If you go into dates unprepared, you are likely to come out with anything. Even in your prayers for a companion, you need to be specific about what you would like the Lord to give you and be careful even in that to ensure you are incorporating your needs, God's will for you and not just what you "want." Because everything we want does not meet our needs.

When employers hire, they do not hire people based on looks, nor do they hire based on charm or how funny you may be, unless you are a comedian or a model. Who they hire is the person who possesses the right combination of skills, experience, and characteristics that will make one not just a good fit for the position, but the best possible option as a long-term fit, as well. You should make no exceptions and do the same.

Interviewers ask you tough questions. They ask you questions that will give them a glimpse of who you are, what your character is like and what type of experiences you have had. They ask questions that will help them recognize, not only if you meet the qualifications for the position, but if you are a good fit for what they are trying to establish within the organization, how you can contribute to the overall vision and help them grow. Why do you not do the same?

On a date question like, "what is your favorite color" or "what is your zodiac sign", do not help you to discover if he or she is your soulmate. As single born-again believers, our hearts should be so hidden in our Father that a person should have to seek Him to find you. In other words, look for the Christ in them, rather than making a life altering decision based on emotions, chemistry, and frivolous conversation. They too should be seeking Christ in you.

Use your dating platform to ask those questions no one really wants to answer, for example, are you saved? If the response is yes, ask them how they know for certain? Find out if they serve in their local assembly, do they believe in tithing and offering, what holidays do they celebrate, what are their core beliefs? Ask about how they grew up. Was there a father in the home or do they come from a single parent background? Are they carrying baggage from past relationships? How did the last relationship end and why? If they blame everything on the other person and accept none of the responsibility, either validate it or run. Ask about children. Do they have children? Do they want children or even like them? Do they take care of their children? How often do they visit their kids? How is the relationship with the other parent?

I know these questions seem forward and intrusive, but they are necessary. You do not have time to waste. You do not need anything delaying or distracting you from bringing your divine assignment into fruition. You need to know if they have goals and the milestones for achieving them. Do they have pets? How do they treat their parents? How often do they visit and spend time and if they do not, then why not? What is your credit score?

If their credit is bad, get an explanation as to why. How long did they spend alone after their last relationship? What did they do during that time? Do they volunteer in the community? Find out how you fit into what they have planned for their life. Ask them how they feel their life glorifies God?

Before you get into their hobbies and the things they do for fun, do not forget to go down the health lane. This person could possibly be your spouse one day and you may want to have children together. Sexually transmitted diseases (STD) are extremely high among our youth and adults. There are people walking around with HIV and AIDS, that will not disclose this information to you, but they will manipulate you into bed and keep on going.

Do NOT become that victim. Instead ask the tough questions. Have you ever had an STD? When was that? Were you treated? How did it happen? Have you been tested for HIV / AIDS? When was the last time? Are you open to us going as a team? Let me just say, the ones who are in it for a quick role in the hay, you will not have to cut. When you have this conversation, they will not call, text, or e-mail you again ever. I know personally from experience.

I have dated men and they passed the interview phase. Then when I asked them if we could go get tested as a team, they would get upset and vulgar. Many times, I have seen men reveal their true character with three simple words, "Let's get tested." That is all right though, because at the end of the day, that is what you want. You want to eliminate anyone who does not want to honor or respect your walk with Christ; therefore, self-elimination is a plus! That candidate just did you a favor by withdrawing their application.

Something else to consider is mental health disorders in the family or personally diagnosed for your potential mate. This is important and not just because you could possibly have children together. This is crucial because if the person suffers with a mental health diagnosis, depending on the severity of the condition, you may or may not be equipped to manage it.

Every question will warrant a response. When those responses are coming out make sure that you are not on Facebook, texting, or involved in any other distraction. Use that platform to ask your questions and listen. Take notes, if you like, on the things you may need to ask follow-up questions about. You may even note the things you want to remember the most, so you can reflect on them later.

Be sure that you pay attention to body language. In listening to the response, you can determine if the person is trying to be evasive. Read the body language to determine if the person is comfortable with the questions. You can make other determinations from body language also. Pay attention to whether they are asking you questions back. This tells you if they are interested in learning more about you and who you are.

In the selection process be sure not to cheat yourself. One-way women and men often cheat themselves is engaging in a relationship with a person who is still technically married. Even if they are separated, they are still married until they are divorced or reconciled. Allow that person to bring closure to their situation. It is not fair to you to be brought into the middle of such circumstances.

Premarital sex is another way you cheat yourself. The world says you need to test the waters to know if you will be sexually satisfied or compatible with a person. This is a bad idea. People need to stop touching what does not belong to them. Sampling the merchandise only creates problems for your flesh. You risk attaching yourself to someone who may not be there tomorrow. Our bodies are members of Christ so we should not connect it to something unholy. The Bible tells us in 1 Corinthians 6:15, *"Do you not know that your bodies are members of Christ? Shall I then take the members of Christ and make them members of a harlot? Certainly not!"*

Therefore, why would you give your body to a person to whom you are not married? When you enter this arena, the flesh will rise because it is natural to be attracted to someone and for the body to have feelings that desire to be touched and crave the companionship of another person of the opposite sex. This is why it is essential not to forget the different biblical strategies that you put in place, while exclusive with God. Being in relationship with God, should have taught you discipline. Therefore, when you try to reintegrate yourself into the dating circuit as a born-again believer, you have to keep that "you are holy" in the forefront of your mind (1 Peter 1:16). *"Your body is a temple for the Holy Spirit which lives in you"* (1 Corinthians 6:19), consequently, you must protect your virtue.

Take Christ into everything, even the dating arena. Remember the instructions of Philippians 4:8-9. Remember to renew your mind as stated in Romans 12:2 - but do so daily. Paul gives us an example that all struggle with sin in Romans 7:15-20 which reads, *"For what I am doing, I do not understand. For what I will to do, that I do not practice; but what I hate, that I do. 16 If then, I do what I will not to do, I agree with the law that it is good. 17 But now, it is no longer I who do it, but sin that dwells in me. 18 For I know that in me (that is, in my flesh) nothing good dwells; for to will is present with me, but how to perform what is good I do not find. 19 For the good that I will to do, I do not do; but the evil I will not to do, that I practice. 20 Now if I do what I will not to do, it is no longer I who do it, but sin that dwells in me."*

We are not exempt to the struggle because we are flesh and blood still but try your best to remain holy. Do not cheat yourself. If for any reason you fail, be quick to repent and do not condemn yourself. God judges us by the intent of our heart. Unlike man, He sees your motives, your desires and what is really inside of you. If your heart's intent is to do the will of God and you fall short, He understands. Repent and live.

Let me be clear on one point, because I do not want anyone to walk away confused and believe that a person is left incomplete without marriage. As you learned in one of the previous chapters some people are designed to be single, although the Bible says it is not good for man to be alone and God created him a helper (Genesis 2:18). The word also says that it is preferred that one would remain unmarried and in the service of the Lord (1 Corinthians 7:7-8). Does that mean that a person will live forever with a void, feelings empty, or "incomplete"? Absolutely not! You were completed when you came into relationship with Christ.

Marriage does not complete us as people, as individuals; rather Jesus Christ does that when He comes into our hearts. Marriage on the other hand completes us in a way unbeknownst to man, the Bible describes it as a great mystery, (Ephesians 5:32). Just as Paul could not explain it, I certainly dare not try. Just know that who God ordains for your life will improve you, not make you worse. A good wife is a gift from the

Lord (Proverbs 19:14). Study these scriptures before making a decision on marriage: Proverbs 31:10-31, Proverbs 12:4, Proverbs 14:1, in addition to Ephesians 5:1-33, Hebrew 13:4 and there are many more. I encourage you to search the scriptures for additional insights into marriage, as many others exist. Familiarize yourself with as many as you can to gain complete understanding before you decide on your life partner, so that you do not settle for less than what God desires for you.

Endure the process. Do not grow weary and settle. Sometimes you may have to get ten no's, before God gives you one yes. That is not because God wants to frustrate you, but He wants you to trust Him, hear His voice and obey Him. Choose to be alone, before you make a decision to yoke yourself to someone that God did not ordain for your life. I understand how tumultuous dating can be. Settling for less than what God wants for you, can result in time wasted and a destiny delayed, while obedience always gets you to the reward expeditiously.

Chapter 10
Nothing Before God

Exodus 34:14
*"For you shall worship no other god, for the LORD,
whose name is Jealous, is a jealous God"*

People have a habit of making other things their God. It can be done knowingly and unknowingly. Women typically put their children before everything in life. This is out of order because not even your children should come before God. When trying to transition from a single person walking in Christ to a dating single in search of companionship, people sometimes lose themselves. They take on the role of a "spouse" far too early and put everything they have into pleasing the other person. In the dating stage, your priority is still God, until you vow, until death do us part.

Let us not misinterpret the word jealous to mean that God is envious because we, as people, have something He wants or needs from us. For example, people envy each other because they see that others may have something they want, or you have achieved something they desired for themselves but have not been successful in doing. This is not the pretense of God's jealousy. He does not envy our material possessions or accomplishments, because these things should be for His glory anyway.

Our God becomes jealous when we give away what rightly belongs to Him to someone else. Examine Exodus 20 verses 4 and 5. It reads: " *You shall not make for yourself an image in the form of anything in heaven above or on the earth beneath or in the waters below. 5 You shall not bow down to them or worship them; for I, the LORD your God, am a jealous God...."*

These scriptures reveal to us that God is dealing with the people on their behaviors of creating and bowing down to idols. These people were worshipping idols, rather than to God. God was jealous because the people had no right to give away what belongs to Him and Him alone, to another who is not worthy of it. Our worship and service belong to Him alone. It is to be given to Him alone, therefore; He is only jealous of what rightfully belongs to Him being offered away.

We can relate this same type of jealousy to marriage. For example, if a spouse has an emotional affair with a person of the opposite sex or an intimate relationship or encounter, and the faithful spouse learns of the indiscretion, they will be jealous and rightfully so. Why do they have a right to be jealous? Because God gave them to each other. Neither have a right to give away any piece of themselves to another person (1 Corinthians 7:3-5). Their relationship is sacred and exclusive, consisting of two, the couple and God. I say two because in the eyes of the creator they are one in the flesh now that they have taken vows with one another.

It is not a sin to experience this type of jealousy. It is all right and expected for you to be jealous over something God has declared to be yours. However, when you begin to envy something that God did not give to you, that is sin. Paul describes the godly jealousy in 2 Corinthians 11:2 - *"For I feel divine jealousy for you, since I betrothed you to one husband, to present you as a pure virgin to Christ."*

Praise, worship, glory, honor, and adoration all belong to our heavenly Father. It is He alone who is truly worthy of all these things. In your time of fellowship with God allow your heart, mind, and soul to truly thirst for Him and His righteousness that you will be filled (Matthew

5:6). Without becoming completely one in Christ you run the risk of being deceived. Your worship and your praise do not belong to men, women, or material things. It does not belong to the Pastor, Evangelist, Preacher, Teacher, Bishop or Apostle; your worship and praise belong to God.

As a single person on the hunt for Christ you will rely on your leaders to help you in the journey. Be cautious not to make them your God. It is all right to honor them for who they are in your life and pay them homage as long as the Christ in them is evident. If the fruit is not evident of a relationship with Christ, then they are not worthy of your respect, but instead need your faithful prayers. Be sure that you are following the Christ in your leader(s) and not following the leader who serves to fulfill his or her own agenda.

The leaders of the body of Christ should be building God's kingdom and not their own. When leaders build God's kingdom, they are effective in helping you as a single individual grow in understanding, grace, and peace. They can assist you on the path of righteous living by holding you accountable in your walk with Christ. Leaders who follow Christ, will develop, and assist you in making your choices towards God's will for your life.

If you put musicians, jobs, vain things, men, women, children, preachers, or teachers before God and begin to worship and/or praise them and not the Father, you have in essence made them an idol in your life. On this journey as a saved and single human being the focus must always be God. Do not seek the church, do not seek the pastor, do not seek the person; merely seek Christ, with your whole heart. Seek the kingdom of heaven and all of its righteousness and everything that you will ever need in this life, in this world shall be added unto you (Matthew 6:33).

Chapter 11
Saved, Single and Solidified in Christ

Isaiah 41:10
"Fear not, for I am with you; be not dismayed, for I am your God; I will strengthen you, I will help you, I will uphold you with my righteous right hand."

This chapter is titled after the text for a specific reason. I want you all to understand its meaning. The title has significance. At this point I will define for you, again, the words that make up the title of this text. There is a blessing in it, and I hope that the preceding chapters have been a blessing to you as well.

Saved is defined as: to keep safe or rescue someone or something from harm or danger. As Christians to be saved is to come into salvation; to be delivered from sin and its consequences, brought on by our faith in Jesus Christ. If we apply the dictionary definition to our situation, Jesus did keep us safe and rescued us not just from our sin, but the consequences we would have had to pay for them, had we not believed.

Our salvation is preservation and deliverance from the ruin sin would bring to our lives.

Throughout the book I have defined what it is to be single. As a refresher, it is said to mean unmarried or not involved in a stable sexual relationship according to the world. As born-again believers, saved, and living a Christ-like life, to be single should obviously mean to be unmarried and in relationship with God. When we are truly saved, we understand that sex outside of marriage is fornication or sin.

Solidify means to make stronger or reinforce; become solid. Initially, I called it Saved, Single, and Solidified for Christ, but then the Holy Spirit spoke to me and said, "you were not saved, single, and solidified for me or in honor of me; but in me through the abiding power of my spirit that I placed in you". He reminded me that He chose me and created me for His glory, and I could not effectively live as a single woman, if it were not for His spirit which dwells within me. To say that we are saved, single, and solidified for Christ, is true, but we would fail miserably, if His spirit is not within.

If we lack the element of salvation, our singleness looks no different than those of the world. There is fornication with no repentance, guilt, or condemnation when we fall short. There is no desire to set things right with God. Instead, we would embrace and actively walk in the sin of the world, remain in a state of confusion, and lose ourselves in life, rather than finding ourselves in Him.

When we bring these pieces of the puzzle together, we learn that we believe in Jesus, so we belong to God (*Saved*). In our single state we are not truly alone because He is with us (*Single*). The power of the Holy Spirit that dwells within us helps us to be successful on the journey, because despite our attempts to resist the temptations life will bring, the Holy Spirit makes us stronger (*Solidified*) and reinforces that Christ is there with us (*In Christ*).

Once we arrive at the place of being saved, single, and solidified "in" Christ there are things that have transpired. We have come into the knowledge of who we are. During our relationship with God, He slowly rebuilds us from the inside out, as we embrace His love and open our hearts and minds to His word. Our faith increases because our study life has improved due to our desire to seek Him. We hear from God when faced with complex decisions now, because we are His sheep, and He is our Shepherd, and we are listening to His voice.

Our eyes are open to how God sees us because we feast on the words of the Bible and digest them and become full. Why? Because we no longer live by bread alone, but every word that proceeds out of the mouth of God (Matthew 4:4). We have an appreciation for Him and have made Him our first love once more (Revelations 2:4), that He may no longer hold our infidelity against us.

You are a part of a chosen generation, a royal priesthood, a holy nation, His own special person, that you may proclaim the praises of Him who called you out of darkness into His marvelous light (1 Peter 2:9); as I have been. Since you pay attention to the commands of the Lord and live them for His glory, you have been made the head and not the tail. You will always be at the top and never beneath (Deuteronomy 28:13). These are promises from God that coincide with our obedience to Christ.

As a saved and single person, your life should be dedicated to His glory. You glorify Him in living out the fruits of the spirit and avoiding the works of the flesh (Galatians 5:19-23). You glorify Him by loving yourself and not settling for a relationship that will not bring Him glory. You glorify Him, by allowing His word to change your mind through the renewal process (Romans 12:2).

Each day you look less like the world, releasing the compromises, customs, traditions, and conformity to the very sin God despises. Rather, you are Saved, Single, and Solidified in Him. You have come into the uniqueness of who you were created to be; your true individualism and represent in every aspect of your person who He has been to you in your life. It is personal now and intimate. In your relationship with Christ, He is your covering, your spouse, your mother, your father, brother, sister, and even at times your only friend. Therefore, enjoy Him during this period and allow Him to be your everything!

Chapter 12
Avoiding the Temptation

1 Corinthians 10:13
"No temptation has overtaken you except what is common to mankind. And God is faithful; he will not let you be tempted beyond what you can bear. But when you are tempted, he will also provide a way out so that you can endure it."

In Chapter Five, *"Using Your Weapons"*, we explored some options that you can implement to prevent yourself from allowing the temptations that are inevitable to come your way, from becoming a manifestation of sin. The opening scripture for this Chapter is also found in Chapter five. I am using it again here to remind you that the word says we will be tempted, but it will not go beyond what is common to mankind and it will not be more that you can handle. In addition to that, He will even provide you with a way out so that you can get through it. Although God provides the way, we must do the work.

In order to avoid temptation, you have to first be real with yourself and acknowledge what your temptations or weaknesses are. There is a possibility that this can be difficult for you as it was for me. How I was able to figure out my temptations was by identifying the areas or hurt, pain, or sadness that existed in my life. Once I knew what those issues were, then I could relate that pain back to a sinful behavior in my life. People do not typically sin for fun. Some do, but most of us do not. Therefore, trace your pain to your sin if you are having difficulty identifying your weakness.

Once you identify your areas of temptation, set goals for yourself to help you overcome them. Make sure that they are S.M.A.R.T., meaning specific, measurable, attainable, realistic and time tied. You may need to adjust the timetables throughout the process. Be sure that you do not do what I did and set goals that are impossible.

For example, one of my issues was anger and I set a goal that I would never curse again. I thought I was doing great, because in casual conversation I was successful in removing curse words from my dialogue. However, because I was not fully healed, I would find myself using profanity in moments of anger or when someone pushed the right button. I would feel bad and beat myself up, get discouraged and then say just forget it. Therefore, you want your goals to be things that are actually possible for you to do that align with where you are in the healing process. You were not messed up overnight; therefore, you probably will not be changed in a day. FYI, I have been delivered from cursing.

Take responsibility for your actions. Do you remember that overlooked fruit of the spirit; self-control (Galatians 5:22). God gives us free will. When faced with your temptation you have the ability to take steps to prevent your temptation from becoming a reality. When Jesus was sacrificed on the cross, He left us with power over the enemy (Mark 16:17) and you have to make every effort to embrace and utilize that power.

Let go of the mistakes of yesterday. I say yesterday because anything that happened yesterday is done and over with; it is the past. You cannot take back the things that you have done in the past. All you can do is recognize those things that were mistakes, learn from them, grow from them, do your best not to repeat them and move forward. The only path from yesterday is today! You cannot go back and change one thing about it; however, you can change right now. You cannot even count on tomorrow because you do not know when Jesus will come, or God will call you home. God has forgiven you, so forgive yourself. Do not carry guilt for something that you have started to correct in your heart.

Change your circle and avoid people and environments that cause you to sin. When you live a life for Christ, not everyone will take you seriously. Everyone will not respect your decision and others will mock you constantly, reminding you of your past. Eradicate those spirits from around you! Some places and some people cause us to be weak. For example, if you are a recovering drug addict, three months clean; you are not going to walk into a crack house, are you?

For me, I had to close the door to a man that I loved, because I knew to be in his presence was to fornicate. I knew he did not respect my desire to live holy and that was because he was content living in sin. By ending our relationship, I eliminated opportunities for sin and temptation. You have to do the same. You know the people and the places that bring out the ungodly behavior. Nip them in the butt and stay away. Do not make them your idols, remember GOD before everything!

We read the scripture earlier in the book that tells us that we overcome by the blood of the lamb and the word of our testimony (Revelations 12:11). What this means is do not be afraid to ask for help. When I truly found God and was still having extreme struggles in my flesh, I felt no one could relate because all the church folks I was around were not transparent. They appeared to have it all together. That is when I learned most Christians lie (no offense).

Do not be afraid to seek help with your struggles. There are good local assemblies out there that are real. They talk to you about the genuine issues you face. They share their testimonies, the journey they went through and how God helped them. Be transparent and do not be afraid to ask for help. God will order the steps of people your way to help you through the process.

Minimize your down time. Tap into the gifts and talents that God has given you and develop them. Set personal goals for yourself. Work on getting closer to God. Work on being a better you. Maybe you want to go back to school, author a book, or start a business venture; whatever it is do it to minimize wasted time. It is like my grandparents used to say, *"an idle mind is a devil's workshop."* You do not have time to entertain the devil. The more of a schedule you have in place to manage your day, the better.

Be consistent in the efforts you make toward overcoming temptation, as it comes. Do not decide to be consistent in one area of temptation, but neglect another, because it can be a secret sin. The world is not who needs to be impressed with your walk, God is. You can pretend in front of people, but God knows all and sees all. I can speak on it because that was me.

I felt like I could keep having sex because no one would know except the man I was having it with, but God exposed my sin and He showed me He was watching. He allowed me to get pregnant. At that moment everyone knew I was not as holy as I was pretending to be. God knew I could never have an abortion, although many hide their shame in this manner, I could not. I charge you to be consistent because anything other than that is not worth it. We cannot hide from God. He does not want us lukewarm. Sin should never be a reward, no matter how good it feels to your flesh.

Accept the fact that temptation is going to come your way as long as you have breath in your body. There will be moments when you fail and sin. In those moments heed the voice of the Holy Spirit and repent quickly, get back on track, forget what is in the past, and move forward. You cannot completely prevent sin, because at moments we do so without even knowing it. You can reduce the exposure you have to certain sins, behaviors, and actions, as well as minimize the hold that temptation has on your life.

You are not perfect and never will be. Come to terms with that quickly or the enemy will use it against you. Do not allow your imperfections to cause you to drop out of the race. There is none perfect except one, Jesus Christ. If you were, what need would you have for Him?

I will conclude with these last thoughts. Continue to focus on your relationship with Christ. Pray and fast, but more than anything else study His word. No good thing dwells in the flesh (Romans 7:18), so you need the word to feed your spirit and your faith, because remember that, *"now faith comes by hearing and hearing the word of God"*, (Romans 10:17). Trust God through the process. Two scripture may help you with this Philippians 1:6, *" being confident of this very thing, that He who has begun a good work in you will complete it until the day of Jesus Christ; being confident of this very thing, that He who has begun a good work in you will complete it until the day of Jesus Christ...", and* Philippians 4:13, *"I can do all things through Christ who strengthens me."*

God is faithful and walks with you through the process. Keep your heart pure because that is how He judges us. Study your word and when you are faced with an issue use it as a weapon. Study the examples of Christ, let Him lead you and guide you on the journey. Let the mind of Christ lead your thinking and the example of His actions in His most holy word, lead your behaviors. Even Christ was tempted. Recall in Matthew 4:2-4, Jesus was tempted - after fasting - to turn stones into bread. However, Jesus was ready and fired back at the enemy with an "it is written." Like Jesus, you will need to be equipped with the word, so when the tempter comes, you too can give him an "it is written" response. Every written word of the Bible is our way of escape and weapon forged with promises.

Acknowledgements

I give Honor to God who is the head of my life. I thank you Father for freeing me from myself, through the power of your Holy Spirit. Thank you for healing me, gifting me, and allowing me the focus needed to complete this divine assignment!

To my children, you are my motivation. Always remember that you can do all things through Christ who is your strength. Pray, focus, and believe. Remember respect, love, and living for Christ always pays off!

To my parents Nathaniel Hopkins and Norma Abdul-Malik, thank you for all you do! Life wasn't perfect, but mom you never gave up. I learned from you both. I love you...

Pedro A. Santos, words cannot express the person you have been in my life. Your heart is big, your character is rare. Allow God to continue to lead you.

Etuwe Otuya, I thank you for allowing me to be who God has called me to be!

Delante Mouton, Jr., Thank you for always being there without judgment. Thank you for keeping me honest and not being afraid to hurt my feelings with the truth and loving me through the process. I appreciate your friendship and your love!

Sheldon "Tim" Curry, I thank you for restoring hope in my life and showing me that people can see you for you and love you for that. It is something I remember and carry with me always!

Saved, Single, & Solidified in Christ

To My sisters Cornette Barfield and Shawn Austin, I thank you for believing in my walk. I thank you for always being willing to help me and hold me accountable to myself and giving me motivation to move forward! Thank you for challenging me also.

To my other sisters Tia Ballenger and Dessie Brown (deceased), we did not choose each other, destiny did and I am pleased with the selection. The bond, the love and the loyalty are like nothing I have ever experienced, but I thank God we are a threefold cord, not easily broken!

My God mother Etta Jalloh, I love you for always having my back.

My Aunt Parice Parker, you were right! A page a day leads to completed work. Thank you for the motivation. I know we do not always agree, but I love you to life, through it all.

Debra and Erick Gordon, you opened the door to a stranger and loved her as your own and as a result of that love, you helped to make me who I am today. You will always be my parents in love. Thank you and I love you so much!

To my family in love Thelma Montique, Aunt Christine Stevenson and Kristal Young, thanks for all the love and support!

Portia Bookhart, Patrick O'Leary, Sr., and Patricia Wright of Cardozo High School, I hope this book reaches your hands one day! I hope that you will know you made a difference in the life of a broken child who has never forgotten you...

About the Author

L. Lorraine Hopkins

Author

Visionary

Teacher / Elder

Motivational Speaker

B.A. - Management

M. Ed - Adult Education and Development

Contact Information:

Twitter: @kolls4god

Facebook: Lorraine Hopkins

E-mail: kolls4god@gmail.com

YouTube: Lorraine Hopkins (Kolls4God)

Address: P.O. Box 464655 Lawrenceville, GA 30042

Ministry Facebook Page: Keeping Our Lights Lit 4 God

Available for purchase on our website: http://www.kolls4god.org

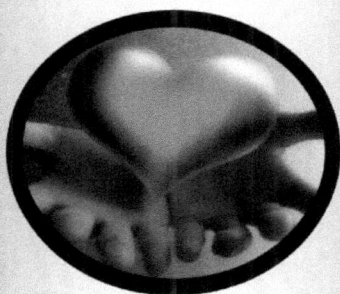

Lorraine Hopkins

Other Books:
Available on: Amazon.com
https://realkchs.square.site
https://kollsministry.square.site
So Many Tears: A Journey for God's Glory

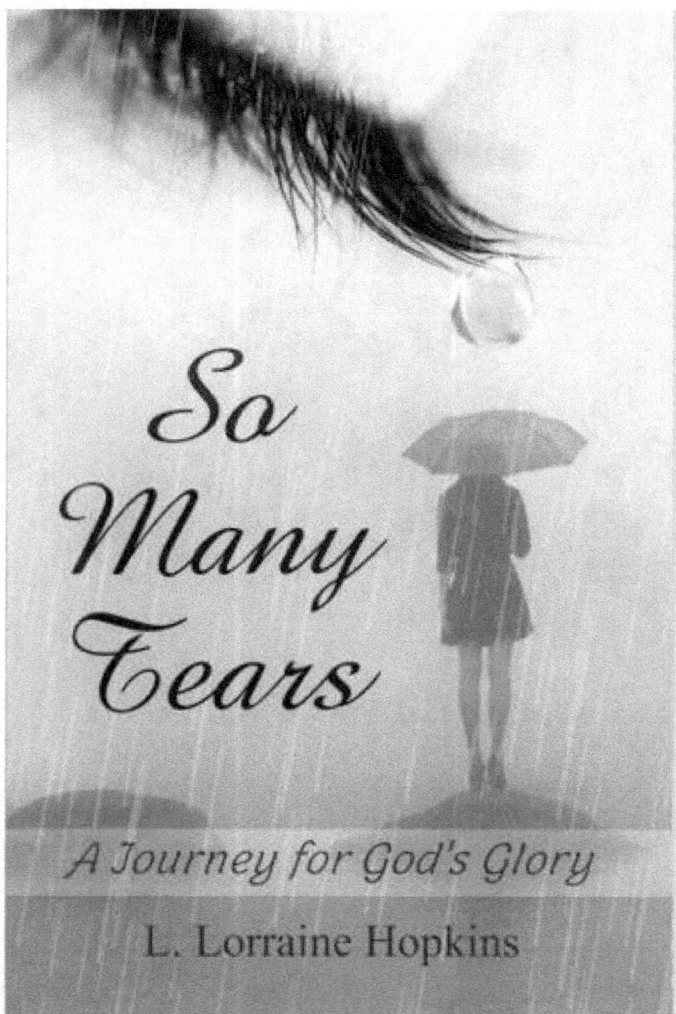